CW00485206

TOUCHED

TOUCHED

Alan Buckley

HAPPENSTANCE

ACKNOWLEDGEMENTS:

Some of these poems were first published in the following: *The Best New British and Irish Poets 2017*, *The Bridport Prize 2012 & 2014*, *The Caught Habits of Language*, *The Compass*, *The Dark Horse*, *Days of Roses II*, *Double Bill*, *Hand Luggage Only*, *Live Canon 2015*, *Magma*, *The Morning Star*, *Oxford Poetry*, *The Rialto*, *Smiths Knoll*, *SMOKE* and *Under The Radar*. Some poems were included in *Shiver* (tall-lighthouse, 2009) and *The Long Haul* (HappenStance, 2016). 'Voicemail' won the 2010 Wigtown Poetry Competition. 'Scum' was highly commended in the 2017 Forward Prizes.

The second stanza of 'Signalman' quotes from Chapter Six of Alexander Frater's book *Stopping Train Britain* (Hodder and Stoughton, 1983). 'Via Negativa' refers to The Fool as portrayed in the Osho Zen Tarot Deck.

Thanks to Sophia Blackwell, Andy Ching, Claudia Daventry, Paul Farley, John Glenday, Lydia Macpherson, Les Robinson, Jacqueline Saphra, Thurlow Road Poetry Workshop, Matthew Turner and Ben Wilkinson for support and comments on poem drafts. Thanks to all the staff, writers, teachers and students I've worked with at First Story. Most poems here were first read publicly at Oxford's Catweazle Club: thanks to Matt Sage and everyone I've met there. In particular, thanks to Helen Mort for her feedback, encouragement and friendship over the last twelve years.

NOTE FOR VISUALLY IMPAIRED READERS:

The main jacket colour is dark purple. On the front cover, all text is centred in the bottom half of the spread: author name first in white italics, followed by a white humming-bird graphic on its own line, then book title in white caps. The back jacket has paler panel of lilac, on which there is a description of the book in black, then an endorsement quote in red. An extract from the poem 'Surrender' (p. 55) appears in dark purple font.

First published in 2020 by HappenStance Press
21 Hatton Green, Glenrothes KY7 4SD
www.happenstancepress.com

ISBN: 978-1-910131-62-6

Printed and bound by Imprint Digital, Exeter
https://digital.imprint.co.uk

CONTENTS

Not this troublous
Wringing of hands, this dark
Ceiling without a star

—Sylvia Plath, 'Child'

BADGER

Glimpsed for no more than a second or two
(I was pushing eighty-five near Stokenchurch Gap)
but enough for a thought to surface: the possibility

that the heft of snout and fur by the central barrier
belonged to a creature that was deaf and asleep,
having nodded off in the morning sun as it looked

for a chance to cross; and this was why it lay there,
oblivious to the cars and lorries bouldering past.
Deaf and asleep, its belly filled with a slither

of worms as it dreamed its brockish dreams,
in which it was busy reliving the night just gone,
when it scuttled through fields of silvery grass

beneath an avuncular moon. And beyond the black,
hard river that carves its way down Aston Hill
a hole in the earth was waiting—a small darkness,

ready to fall back behind this animal's tail, like
the heavy curtain at the entrance to a private room,
shielding from view a silent, untouchable space.

LIFE LESSONS

How do I live with grief and madness?
By telling yourself it's your fault.

How do I live when my needs are punished?
They're locked in a faraway vault.

How do I live without being touched?
Your skin will become stainless steel.

How do I learn to survive in a vacuum?
Don't move. Don't breathe. Don't feel.

JUNCTION

For us, the actual weather doesn't matter.
Today the sky's cloudless, an impossible
blue remembered from childhood holidays,
our pure movements lit by a final sun.
Everything shows its beauty—a murky
canal, a screeching bird, a thorny tree—
and yet is growing separate, the way
two trains diverge. Fields slowly expand

filling the space in between. We see faces
of friends, lovers, family pressing on
carriage windows, shrinking to dabs of pink.
A day of clear focus, parallel rays
drawn down through a lens to a burning point.
Spring is in our veins, as we test a coil
of rope for strength, or tuck damp towels
into the gaps around a garage door.

GRAVITY

The aerialist swings out, hair rippling,
beyond the proscenium arch. Just below
the dead point, where upward force
and downward pull are perfectly matched,
she lets go—we gasp—of the *corde volante*,
and there, for a heartbeat, body and rope
are floating apart. Later, she'll smile:
*Whatever you choose to think, I cannot fly. I fall
professionally.* But the woman above us now
is not the one with tied-back hair, calloused
hands, who carefully checks the shackles
and silks before the audience comes. She
has vanished, as we all have, briefly released
from our fragile, desperate weight.

PEACHES

Truly they're God's own fruit, glowing
like little suns. We name their juice *nectar*.
Apples and pears can't rival their tender
beauty. And yet they struggle, don't know
how to handle the market's jostle. They keep
to themselves, try and avoid the mêlée
of bruising fingers. Then a careless nail
nicks the velvety blush, leaves them weeping.

No wonder so many evolve, adapt.
Their view is opaque, tightly curved.
We knock on the tin. Perhaps they're asleep?
They can't be touched. In their dark world
they sit motionless, doped with syrup,
not sure if they're hiding or trapped.

PSYCHOTHERAPY

Summer of '86. Still a student, before
the wilderness years of my twenties,
the groping towards a 'career',
and me and a friend had blagged our way
to New York. We saw them perform
off-Broadway—Penn all spiel and patter,
Teller his mute sidekick. Back then
it was novel, deconstructing magic
in front of an audience. To close the show
Penn delivered a monologue on eating fire.
How d'you not burn your mouth?
—that was what people always asked him

and his big reveal was this: *There is*
no trick. You do burn your mouth,
especially to begin with. What's more,
each time you do the act you swallow
some lighter fluid. It makes you nauseous,
slowly poisons your liver. No matter:
his explanation just deepened my sense
of wonder. He paused, as if to gather
his thoughts, then shifted his gaze, and I swear
his eyes were focussed on mine. *Magic*
is fake. Sideshow skills are real. You shouldn't ask
how we're doing this, but why.

ALBUM

—June 3rd, 1955

Front and back covers, the card facing
each photograph: completely white.
Only the opening page has text—
bride and groom, church, date,
bridesmaid, best man. Everything
else is space, in which to write
new chapters, a different life.

Wait. The old stories are blurred
figures, lost in the snow. They gather,
clamour at my lit windows, palms
outstretched, beg to be fed with words.
They will go back, they promise me,
to wherever they came from.
But first they need to be heard.

COWLEY ROAD, 12.20 PM

A dozing baby
snug in a sling

on its mother's breast
as she pedals along.

A double-decker
six feet behind her.

Sun glints off the spokes
which are perfectly tense.

SPLIT

I'm both—the one who resurrects
and also the corpse, wrapped
in white linen. I stare
at the bedroom curtains

as dawn leaks in at their edges.
My mind's a tomb, shut
with a boulder, beyond
which the other me weeps.

Sometimes we pull it off,
give the punters a show.
I strut my stuff on the big stage.
But mostly there's no miracle,

just compromise, days spent
in a café off the main drag,
our coffees cooling before us.
We've so much, so little to say.

Our hands are beached fish
that twitch on the table.
If someone could only move
that ketchup bottle, who knows,

they might even touch.

THE STORY OF THE PLATES

My father, who for years had made a pantomime fuss
when my mother, serving dinner, handed him plates
that had sat in the oven for half an hour, on this
particular day went off like a bomb before he burst
into tears saying *Don't tease me. Please don't tease me*—
and it was only then, after forty years of marriage,
that he told her what had happened, which she in turn only
told me long after he died, this story I'm telling you now.

But in order to tell it I have to go back to when my
grandad—a widower with a young son, his wife killed
by the flu pandemic after the Great War—meets my nan,
who's twenty, and there's a fiery attraction between them.
One weekend the three of them visit Llandudno
along with my nan's sister, who's meant to be acting
as chaperone, but at night my half-uncle hears the click
of doors, floorboards groaning, he knows what's going on.

The shame. The hurried wedding. My nan with a baby
and boy to care for, and a husband who wakes up screaming,
his body convulsing, his head full of nightmares he can't
find the words to describe. And he has these accidents
at work, like his mind is somewhere else. She thought she'd made
a good catch—a mill manager, the owner's son—but they keep
demoting him, he's just not up to it. This isn't what
she'd dreamed of, and that baby—my dad—is to blame.

My father's five. He's in the living room; I can picture it
from Sunday visits when I was a kid. He's poking the fire
around when my nan comes in. She gets down behind him,
grabs his wrists, and forces his hands to within an inch
of the pulsing coals. Not touching—just above. He squirms
but she doesn't let go. I can see them there, but I can't
hear anything. Most films were silent back then: you had
to imagine what people were saying, the sounds they made.

TRUTHS

Alan was the brother my nan was closest to,
and she assumed I'd been given that name
in memory of him, so treated me

more favourably. My parents denied it,
but every story's like a spell—when someone
in another room calls me he always appears.

He's young, late teens at most: shoulders back,
parade-ground smart, his cap badge
a third eye, Brasso-ed to a spotless shine.

His uniform's free of mud, and there's no trace
of the trenches' piss-rot stink. His God-fearing,
virginal body intact. Even the War Office smoothing

('died of his wounds') was more than his mother
could bear; she made him a victim of influenza
when the truth is a shell blew off both of his legs.

It took him three days to die, strapped to a bed
in a field hospital. My namesake turns to me.
Think of me at my best, he says. *That's all I ask.*

ANUSOL®

Although she dropped by without warning, conversation
was easy until she came back from the bathroom. I felt
the air heavier, thickened with embarrassment. Later,

I saw the tube where I'd left it, perched on the edge
of the tub: that blunt, un-English name, the manufacturer—
Canadian—unaware of our sensitivities. Please understand:

we are born uncomfortable. We must apologise for these
bodies that block up our narrow streets, that brush
and bump in Underground trains. We have smoked them

brown as kippers, stuffed them with pig fat until they drip,
soaked them in cheap gin; and yet they persist, refuse
to go away. We wish they would show some decency

and do what they do behind closed doors. We want
to be left on our own, with only our monkey-house minds
for company, the chatter and scream of our thoughts.

GRESHAM'S LAW

It's four in the morning. My heart wants
to escape from my chest, the sheets are damp
with sweat, and it seems like this terror's come
out of the blue. I travel back to 1965,
and I'm foetal, floating in that space
where all life's currency is hammered out.
Every cell in my body's a bright planchet
struck with a sorrowful face, monarch
of that strange country I'm going to enter.
The law of the land is Gresham's Law: *Bad money
drives out good.* I'm the shadow-twin of Croesus,
about to be born with the anti-Midas touch,
all gold turned to lead. This is my inheritance.
However hard I try, it's never spent.

TWO SHIPS

We take the madman off to a seaside town,
me and the Russian, hire a chalet near
to the beach. A last-chance saloon: either
we bring him back from his blank world—persuade,
implore, cajole—or else we have to leave him,
shuffling round his strip-lit ward with marble
eyes, hummingbird hands. He gives us hell,
ram-bamming doors, smashing plates. He slops
and spills his food, smears it over his clothes,
whines for smokes and milky, four-sugared tea.
Come the second night, we're hopelessly frayed,
a single strand away from breaking point.
It's my turn to sleep in his room. I make
my way to bed with burglars' steps. We're close,
no more than a couple of yards between
our skulls, his breathing as loud as my own.

A vivid dream. I've given away my house.
The front door's ajar... I push it open.
Inside, unfamiliar faces leer
from semi-darkness, flushed with drink. I find
a telephone, open my address book.
Cover to cover, every page nameless,
white as hospital sheets... I wake with a jolt,
half-paralysed, clutching the edge of the bed.
The Russian's up and gone, taking the madman
out to the sands. At midday they return,
walking reverend-soft, wrapped in stillness,
their shoulders dropped. The Russian shakes his head:
I can't believe it. Look at him, quiet
as a mouse, and all he'll say is that he had
this dream last night—he'd given away his house,
found it full of strangers, shouting and drunk...

The madman smiles at me and lifts his hands—
Two ships, he whispers, *just a pair of ships*
at sea in the night; moves them, slow and precise
in a closing V, until the fingers touch.
And I can see that intimate collision,
hear the howl of steel in crumpling bows.
The vessels slide below the surface, sink
a third, two-thirds, a mile, until a double
douff—primordial silt enfolds them both,
gathers them into the gloom. The sea calms,
gradually unclouds. The glimmering fish
appear, with global eyes and popping mouths,
streaming their bubbled wakes. They flick and shiver
through the wrecks, and slip down funnels, out
of portholes, find the gaps in splintered decks,
making this pair of hulks a single home.

MR AND MRS CLARK AND PERCY

—David Hockney, 1970-71, acrylic paint on canvas

I like the way you capture that chic milieu—
Ossie's chrome-frame chair, the white telephone
casually untabled on the carpet, Celia's
purple smock dress. And I like how I'm shown
too much, the genre subverted: husband seated,
not wife; no flow of gaze from one to the other
to viewer, but both facing me from either
side of the window's gulf. I'm made complicit,
a triangle's third point. But what I love is the cat,
Blanche, given Percy's name; you decided that
was artistically correct. Back turned to me it sits,
slender and erect, on Ossie's faithless lap,
staring out at something beyond all this
deceit, at something beyond my grasp.

KAREN

Loneliness is such a sad affair
  —The Carpenters, 'Superstar'

Half a dozen musicians on stage
but the camera is hungry only for her,
cheekbones sharp as a cracked wafer,
eyelids chlorine blue beneath the untouchable
gloss of her fringe. The oboe part is the fall
of a dying swan: every instrument—from
muted horns to sparse and elliptical bass—
follows her lead of consummate restraint,
vibrato exquisitely sustained, its modulation
just so. No histrionics, no push to an upper
octave. Those lips have a high-hat's default
to a thin closure, and only what's strictly

required may pass. Between first chorus,
second verse, the camera drops back, before
closing in again. She stares at nothing,
shuts her eyes, and turns her head away
a fraction. Her face is the face of a girl
sitting on a bed, who doesn't cry—
not through fear of an adult's response
but knowing no adult will come.
Then the singer returns, delivers *that* line.
She executes her professional trick,
convincing us that someone else's words
are her own, that what she sings is for real.

CLINICAL

I stretch my lips, and make a large red O.
You tease an angled mirror into place.
Dispassionate voyeur, I feel
your sickle probe, its pick and scrape.
Another old absence needs to be refilled.
You prick my gums into a little death,
then wait. The lamp's mesmeric, draws
my unblinking stare up past your face,
concealed with clinical cap and mask.

I hear a drill being startled into life.
Stranger, with a lover's close gaze, this
is the hidden room where all my words
are given shape, before I set them free.
But you are single-minded and read nothing
there, except the story of my decay.
Please let me hear your soothing voice.
Tell me when I can eat and drink again.
Tell me when the numbness will go.

UNDER

You wander into a country pub, somewhere
near the middle of England. You see me
at a family gathering—I'm uncle, brother, son.
The mains have just arrived: flurries of chatter
criss-cross the table over the restless squeal
of knives on plates. You can tell I'm distracted,
not wholly part of the group. Forgive me.
I'm afraid small talk isn't my strength.

I'm sorry for my solemn tone, my gravity.
A river, unmentioned by everyone here, flows
underground beneath this familiar terrain.
For better or worse, I'm a forked branch of hazel,
a pair of L-shaped metal rods. I twitch,
pull away from you. It's nothing personal;
I'm drawn by a stronger force. And yet (I see
it puzzles you) I make no move to leave.

It's like this. I can sense that somewhere
below there's the arch of an aching cavern,
a lake formed by the warm salt water
rising up from its source. But each time
I set out to go there I come to that other place
where the river bursts from the hillside
into clear light. I see his body washed up
on a gravel spit — a boy, no age at all.

I recognise his sodden duffle coat, his dripping,
skull-cap hair. Here's where I always stop.
I know I need to meet his gaze, its emptiness,
with mine. Until I can, he will not let me pass.

THE VANISHING

pillowcases   filled with presents
hand-drawn nametags
attached with safety pins
variety packs of cereal
on the breakfast table   all
        easily summoned

but not the Christmas Day
when I was five   your mind
gave way   you vanished
the police went looking for you
you ended up
        on a psychiatric ward
I can't remember this

I only found out in my forties
my brother told me   everything
made sense   how after
I'd left home   each year
when the clocks went back
        the anxiety began
creeping in   my mood darkening

I knew I didn't want
to go home for Christmas
my body's clock had spun
back   to that five-year-old boy
what he felt
        couldn't be blanked out

although I remember once
when I was older   I found
a bottle of pills   in the room
you called your study
        you walked in on me
I braced myself for your anger
there was no anger   you shrank

dropped your head
          neither of us spoke

years on   I want to show you
this   the packet of tablets
I'm holding
          it's my name on the label

from the moment the waters break
we're swimming all our lives
          swimming for dear life
trying not to go under
our arms grow tired   we cling
to whatever might keep us afloat

DINOSAURS

Earth's the right place for love:
I don't know where it's likely to go better
    —Robert Frost, 'Birches'

With great intent you test your toddler's legs
against this cattle-carved ground, the weather
remarkably mild for New Year's Day. Across
the valley, Easdon Tor seems an eternal
sentinel. There's no low hum of traffic,
no vapour trails stretching out above us,
and we might imagine our print on the land
is slight—the moss-greened walls tumbling down
the slopes, the narrow lanes, white cottages,
a slow accretion over hundreds of years.

Your legs decide they've had enough for now.
You stop and wobble, raise your arms. Your dad
responds by lifting you onto his back.
You're clutching a plastic dinosaur, whose name
(*Tyrannosaurus Rex*) you announce with pride.
You've not yet learned what 'extinction' means.
Everything you see is new and bright,
unshadowed by what we know. It's topsy-
turvy, Ozzie B. It should be you
who makes a mess, and us who clean it up.

We reach the gateway at the common's edge.
You've come a long way, scarcely bigger
when you were born than the toy that's in your hands,
and though what helped you stay was frenzied skill
and that great anchor, love, I need to believe
there's some exceptional longing for life
in you, a superhuman push of blood
that finally planted you here. Godson,
we need you to be godlike. Forgive us
this day the weight we place on your shoulders

THE ELEMENTS

—i.m. Hussain Mohammed

Cycling home, gone ten,
I'm brought back down to earth.
Boys keep vigil on the bridge.
The river took their friend,

his breath. It acted without love
or spite. Now railings vanish
underneath a surge of flowers,
bunched and wrapped.

A hundred tea lights laid out
on the pavement spell
his name. Each burns away
some tiny piece of night.

SCRIPT

You rhyme with *clean, machine.*
You've come to purge my body
of its early morning fear.
These words stick in my throat.
For years I've tried to live
without you, stubborn as hell,
as if I'd something to prove.

Not suffering in silence goes
against the grain. I raise
a glass to my lips and swallow
both my pride and you—
a tablet with a little
groove, easily snapped
in two. Just like a brain.

LANDICAN

Here's where they burned
my nan, my father.

Though ice defined them,
what bound them was fire.

HOW THEY GOT BACK TO MURMANSK

After his son's wedding, the shell
of my grandad's body drives his wife
back home, north to the greying air
and dark red terraces, past the tall-chimneyed
mill he once ran. The core of him
is two thousand miles and decades away,
an English soldier sent to support
the White Army fighting the Reds.

*

He's on the ship bound for Murmansk,
the waves so high the captain calls
for the priest, instructs him to give
every man the last rites, Catholic,
Protestant, Jew. Below decks
Father O'Halloran braces himself
between the hand-rails flanking
a flight of steps. He offers them all
viaticum, food for the journey,
the body and blood of Christ.
It may not do you much good, boys,
but it surely won't do you any harm.

*

He's marching through an alien land,
the winter so bitter it snaps
rifle barrels in two. The peasants,
their flag tied to the Bolshevik cause,
refusing to share their thin soup,
black bread. Politicians call this
The North Russia Intervention.
The soldiers call it *a fool's errand.*

*

He's on the slow retreat to the sea.
Not bullets killing his comrades but
hunger, cold and hunger. Shovels clang
on frozen earth. More graves to dig.
Someone—he can't remember who—
looks at a corpse, and speaks the unspeakable
thought. Everything else he recalls
clearly: the way time seems to be stopped,
until an officer nods his grim assent.
The face of the private they fetch,
a butcher by trade back home.
The smell of it being cooked. The taste.

THE ERROR

They're standing like figures on a cake, by a pre-war
Hillman Minx. My father, stiff as the mannequin his suit
was lifted from, has a pleasantly startled expression
as if he can't quite believe he's got to this threshold
beyond which adult life begins. My mother's hiding
behind her lipstick smile, the blinding white
of her dress. They think they've found a way out,
and here's the car that will take them away
to a housing estate that's still being built, to earth
that's yet to be dug over to make a vegetable patch,
to a life untethered from its past. They're wrong,
of course; I'm witness to how their histories
followed them out of this frame. But look—here's
where I'll choose to say I come from, that small
place of reassurance that something else is possible,
the warm hollow made by their locked hands.

PIP

After her phone call, I can't be casual
about this act—the two angled slices
into each half of the pear, to remove
the core before poaching. I scoop you out
with the nail of my little finger, black seed
dreaming of what you'll become. She's asked me
to godparent something no bigger than you,
a cluster of cells inside her, and offer
it some guidance, although by the time I meet
her/him eye to eye they'll have found the basic
shape of life without any help from me.
What can I tell you, Pip? Too much perspective
may prove to be bad for your health. You're just one
among billions. You're one in a million.

SHERBET LEMONS

Out of reach, high
in a wall of glass jars.
The newsagent clambers
up steps. Bitter pearls,

rattled onto scales, slid
into a white paper bag.
I feel their stickiness,
hold one up to the light.

It glowers back, a sour
eye. The shine defies
my milky teeth: I work
my tongue, slither

and roll, until the shell
relents with a crack.
A startle of yellow fizz:
I think of her, late at night

in a room I'll never see,
unleashing that shock
of blonde. How it shivers
down her naked back.

LAST NIGHT OF THE WRITING RESIDENTIAL

The pupation phase is not of fixed length, and may
continue for weeks, months, or even years
  —C. G. Barrett, 'The Lepidoptera of the British Islands'

Eighty teenagers: each one takes the stage
to their peers' applause. One dares to speak
her lover's name—*Juliet, I am your Romeo*—
defying her parents' disapproval.
Another says how her fingers feel in her throat,
how still the toilet water is before
the vomit hits. A third describes the scars
that swarm all over her arms and thighs, turning
from red to white. She calls them *butterflies*.

They put me to shame, me with my clever craft
and measured restraint, though it's nothing
compared to the shame I felt at their age,
bowing my head to the men who taught me
my body was there to be pawed at, punished.
The only safe place I had was enclosed
by the book-lined walls of my mind.
What can the wrongly-desired body do
but harden, as if it were a chrysalis?

Tonight, layers are being shucked off. One
by one the writers emerge. A question
flares above us: *If not now, then when?*
My teenage self is in the audience
clutching a sheet of paper. He gets to his feet,
hesitates, sits down, and all the hands
in this packed room can't lift him up. He crushes
himself back into his seat. Poor kid.
He's learned how risky it is to be seen.

CLOCKS

Saturday morning breakfast at the Tick Tock Café
has become a habit of late. Reassuringly old school:
walnut-effect Formica tables and red banquettes;
tabloid papers; a healthy emphasis on food that's toasted
or fried. And that eponymous quirk, the walls covered
in clocks, though it's only today I'm getting the resonance,
the chime (can you forgive the pun?) as I think back
to that July day, down in your home town on the coast,
visiting your grandad. I'd acquitted myself pretty well,
been introduced to his plump rabbit and skittery ferrets,
the girlfriend half his age he'd met at the day centre,
and we'd all of us gone to his front room to sit and drink tea.
We'd been in there for a good long while when I saw,
from the corner of my eye, it was twenty past five,
then glimpsed another clock, a couple of feet away,
six minutes slower. I was pondering the discrepancy
when it struck me—*the room was full of fucking clocks.*
There were dozens of them, cheap and tacky clocks ticking
their tocks in plastic splendour. Mickey Mouse. 'A Gift
from Bournemouth'. Elvis's hips, forever thrusting in time.

We stepped out into the light, as if from a matinee.
What's with the clocks? I said, and you replied *They help him
not to feel alone*, matter-of-fact, like it was no big deal.
After we'd broken up, I put it all into a poem,
but I couldn't finish it. I kept reworking the last lines
but nothing felt right, though there had to be an ending
somewhere, I thought, if only I searched for it long enough.
Part of me thinks you could walk in here right now,
all bustling swagger, never mind it's twelve years further on,
and seven years since I stood on a beach, and watched
your ashes being thrown to the waves. You place your order,
and we talk. It's there, that endearing half-twitch of a smile,
you're teasing me in a way that's not wholly playful,
and I don't know quite how to respond, as I feel that great
mixed bag of emotions all over again. You ask me,
as you did once before, *What happens when an unstoppable*

force meets an immoveable object? Maybe, with patience,
both might be altered for the better, in some small way.
Or maybe we can't be anything other than this—
face to face, surrounded by clocks, but out of time.

HIS FAILURE

December 31st. Almost a year without cigarettes.
Fear of death had done the trick. At the party, I met
Elena: she smiled, and the gap between her front teeth
only made her more beautiful. She offered me
a Marlboro Light, then lifted her foot, struck a match
off the scuffing on the sole of her black
stiletto. I tell you, I pulled so hard on that filter
I nearly sucked in the whole damn universe. I felt
like a god. No—scrub the indefinite article—
like God. My hangover, though, was two days of hell.

But no regrets. To fall short of perfection
is to leave a necessary space. Take the temptation
of Gawain, how in the end Bertilak's foxy lady
got him, despite his chivalric codes and priggish piety.
He came back all boo-hoo and tail between his legs,
her bright green girdle slung over that nick on his neck,
and crazy with shame—he heard Camelot's laughter
as a monstrous choir, confirming his failure.
Didn't get it, how they truly welcomed him home;
welcomed him, finally, as one of their own.

CONFESSIONAL

'I knew these people'
  —Harry Dean Stanton as Travis Henderson in *Paris, Texas*

Maybe this is like that booth—
I'm Harry Dean Stanton and
you're Nastassja Kinski. You
can't see me, and my back's turned
towards you, as I husk out
these words into the white phone.
You hear my disembodied
voice through the little speaker.
Love. Obsession. Alcohol.
Jealousy. You smooth your hair:
your grey eyes flicker and fill
with tears. You realise this
story's not just about me.

Or maybe I'm Nastassja.
Though you think you can see me,
make-up's the heart of my trade.
I'm only ever who you
want me to be. I kneel down,
and press my hands to the glass
of the one-way mirror. But
when you turn, it's your ghost face
that's staring back at you, framed
by my blonde hair. Look at that
white space. In a couple of
lines, you'll drive off into it,
believing we really met.

PORNOGRAPHY

He's come, he says, to the conclusion that what
does it for him, nine times out of ten, is brunettes.
Medium-length brown hair, perhaps skimming
her collarbones, or falling part way down between
her shoulder blades, though not too long. Or too straight,
ideally; at least a hint of wave and curl. Brown hair
and large breasts. No particular shape, but large,
and a slim waist. He prefers some narrative too,
however ridiculous. In fact, the more ridiculous
the better, so that no one could fail to be in on the joke,
and under cover of this caricature the real illusion
can be smuggled—the availability, the invitation to gaze
without shame, to touch, penetrate, merge. Of course,
I say, there's no actual connection; between him
and the softly moaning woman there's always a screen.
He shrugs. I ask the obvious question; he hesitates.

He's a small boy. He can't remember exactly
what age, but he's older than five and younger
than ten. He's looking through the open door
of his parents' bedroom. His mother is naked apart
from her white pants. She sits on the edge of the bed,
like a woman in a painting by Degas or Bonnard
he says, putting her tights on, head forward.
She's focussed on her feet, she seems not to know
that he's there. He senses he shouldn't be doing this.
I ask what happens next and he says nothing
happens. They're motionless, both of them are inside
the painting, the boy standing on the swirly-patterned
carpet, the woman, with light streaming in
from beyond her, halfway through pulling on
the rolled-up nylon. It's strange, he says, for the life
of him he can't think what colour her eyes are.

MATRYOSHKA

The largest one (containing
all the rest)
may be the only one you'll see.
Serene. Polished.
That lively expression
is your own, reflected back.

If you're patient
and lucky
you might hear a squeak
as the halves are eased apart.
More than a smaller copy.
Fractional changes—look,

such subtle brushwork.
Almost the curve of a smile.
Then, if the sun
has really warmed the air,
if the ghosts aren't here
whispering in the shadows...

But not today. Hollowness
is all I know.
Perhaps there's nothing
inside but dreams.
That tiny kernel,
solid as a pumping fist?

If it was ever there, it's lost.
Someone
has been neglectful.
It gathers dust,
wedged behind a bookcase
or crying softly beneath a chair.

THE WELL

Like a boy
dropping stones
down a well
I write these words
into your absence

All I can hear
is a far-off splash
a tiny echo

Where is your voice
Father
that tells me
when to stop
that tells me
the game is over?

THE RAILWAY CHILDREN

'Daddy! My Daddy!'
 —Jenny Agutter as Bobbie, in the 1970 film of *The Railway Children*

You saw from when I was young that during our holidays
I could, without any fuss, be left all day at a station
or even somewhere overlooking a railway line,
while my brother fished and you and my mum
went sightseeing. I knew already alone was different
from lonely. I was happy watching the passing trains
with their yellow ends and flat blue livery,
their grudging chunter and plumes of grey exhaust.
August '73: high-looping seagulls spiral down,
squabble over dropped ice-creams, half-eaten bags of chips.
Shrieks and squeals ripple out from the beach.
Signal wires swish taut, the lofty red-and-white arms
swing upwards, and I gaze at the uniformed man
in his box, standing behind his bright levers.
Growing up I wanted to be him, to live
in his ordered, separate world. By then I'd exiled
you and your flashpoint rage, your despair's black
vacuum. I learned the cold art of steeling myself,
and when you came up in conversation I referred
to you with an edge of formality as *my father*.
Even your death didn't wholly soften my voice.

Now I'm watching that film again. I'm not paying
attention to Perks's birthday, the landslide, the runner
who trips in the tunnel. I'm waiting for that scene,
three minutes before the end. It's me on a platform
high in the West Yorkshire hills, as a train of Edwardian
carriages—all gold letters and intricate panelling—
draws away. The engine has shrouded the station in steam,
a theatrical mist from which you emerge, hat in hand,
wearing a black greatcoat, not only the man you were
but the man you could have been, that you wanted to be.
I find myself running towards your open arms,
and the word I'm gasping isn't close-lipped *father*—
it's not that word, it's not that word at all.

ALL THAT MATTERS

Once, he imagined it like this.
A hillside, miles from the nearest
town, the ground hard and brisk
with frost, the night sky clear,
blue-black as the bottle of ink
on his desk. Two people
covered by a rough wool blanket,
hot from the reckless rush of sex.
The firewood pulsing orange-red,
dying down towards charcoal,
eager sparks flicked out and up
into the cool, still air. They lie there
naming the constellations,
their throats raw with the peat
and iodine burn of a single malt,
gulped from an antique flask.

But he's older now, with something
that passes for wisdom, so winter
is a dull warfare of lightboxes,
St John's Wort, against the shrinking
days, and as the solstice draws near,
with its promise of what will return,
at least he knows this—the sweating
murmur of two familiar bodies,
crumpled under a duvet's drift.
A boiler flares. The house gurgles,
ticks, stretches towards the morning.
All that matters is the recognising
touch, one skin finding its home
in the other. Later, they might dress,
walk out for coffee at some café
down the road; or maybe not.

KAI

Your name's the tree-top rasp
of a raven's call.
Your heart had learned how to fly
before you could crawl.

Your twin brother's King of the World.
You're the Lord of Misrule.
Though your spirit's dressed in motley
you're nobody's fool.

SEVEN STEPS ON THE WAY

Everything is nothing, but afterwards.
After having suffered everything
  —Antonio Porchia

i
Carpe Diem. The guru laughs.
Regrets make feeble epitaphs.
I feel ashamed. Dusk draws near
and I still haver, seized by fear.

ii
At the rave of existential angst
I'm DJ Eeyore, lost inside my trance,
sorted for unease and sad for it.
I think you think my gold disc sounds like shit.

iii
Trauma makes us refugees
from our own lives. Our bodies
become a hostile environment.
We pray for permanent resettlement.

iv
Although I know my task—to love my fate—
my fate's not clear. Which path should I take?
I spread the cards. I scan them fruitlessly.
I anagram my name: *Bleak Lunacy.*

v
I focus hard. The flames are bright,
but I don't feel myself catch light.
I drop down into my black heart.
I've no choice but to make a spark.

vi

Bishop: the great disguised Confessional.
When she says that *Somebody loves us all*
I hear a child's longing, not belief.
A mother locked up. An absence. Grief.

vii

I learned how to negotiate
with pain, and quit that subtle opiate
whose soothing helped me cope.
I'd stayed unborn by living in hope.

THINGS CAN ONLY GET BETTER

Though the building's long since demolished,
the land redeveloped, let's pretend
we can walk back through the yellow dining room
into the garden, each of us carrying
a mug of sweet tea, you with your Spar
own-brand Superkings, me with my tin
of Golden Virginia. We sit cross-legged
on the grass. T-shirt weather. We're in
the pink cloud of New Labour's honeymoon,
the memories fresh—that song blaring out
at a fist-pumping rally; that winsome,
winning smile; *A new dawn has broken*
outside Number 10. And now those images
flooding our TV screens—a dead princess
in an underpass, Kensington Palace
adrift on a sea of flowers. A country
at ease with showing its tears, the old ways
losing their hold. We draw on our cigarettes
and exhale, hazing the late summer air.
It seems like nothing lies out of reach.

We talk about ordinary stuff. What
you might go on to do, one day. Study.
Get a job. Even have your own family.
Lieben und arbeiten, das ist alles
and who cares if Freud never actually
said this? Ordinary stuff, as if the years
to come were blank pages in a journal
that we might fill however we wanted.
As if the hand has no compulsion
to write what it's written before.

SPIRITS OF THE DEAD

Having been taken to Christchurch Meadow
to get to know more of the city, he spotted
a horde of them cawing and strutting
their sheened blackness. In his country
people believe they're the spirits of the dead,
come back to watch over the living.

He's telling me this with a childlike fervour,
and in return I'm feeling warmly paternal,
so I can't help but mention his father—
a farmer, killed because of his too-brown skin
during the civil war, although *We were lucky.*
They told us where we could find his body—

and he says yes, he was thinking as he stood
on the meadow that one of these birds
might well be his father, who'd followed him here
to this uncomfortable country, where now
the days hang stiff with frost, and people huddle
themselves in wool, stomping their feet at bus stops.

As for my own father—who said, before he died,
he'd never really known what it felt like
to be loved—with his sharp nose and gleaming
eyes, he'd fit in well with the crows.
I think he might find among them a sense
of belonging, of something he could call home.

Later I meet him, perched on the washing line
outside my flat. He tells me what I know already,
that some people spend all their lives in search
of a refuge. For them, the sparrow that flits
through the mead-hall feels in an alien space,
and exiled—for now—from the true and beautiful dark.

SCUM

—Hillsborough, 15.04.1989

I lay on the turf, under a steely sky.
No one picked my pockets. No one pissed
on me. The copper who gave me the kiss
of life wasn't beaten up. I died,
that's the truth; and though I'd never known
such closeness—our bodies like beans in a can—
when the air was squeezed from me I died alone.

That's all changed. The words we sang as fans
became our bond. We've walked, the ninety-six,
through parish halls, hushed stadiums, and courts.
Now we walk back through time. Something sticks
in our throats. You're at your desk, lost in thought,
scanning a page of lies you'll say is true.
What's the headline that can trumpet this?

Look up. We're standing right in front of you;
what burns in us is fierce as any sun.
That word you want to use. It's on your lips.
Say it to our faces, one by one.

SURRENDER

Civil war is a national crisis and also a private
trauma: we suffer it collectively and in isolation
  —Hisham Matar

The men whose stories I've listened to today
have known how it feels to be half-human,
half-automaton, a rifle stock jammed
in their armpit, trigger finger applying
precisely not quite the pressure required.
They've known how it feels to stride towards
a body that might or might not belong
to an innocent bystander, a body
they scan, watching for a hint of movement.
They wonder, as I do, how they'll be healed,
when here and now is also there and then.
Their stony vigilance seems as though it'll
never end, and I've no words to disarm them.

It's 7.40 pm and I'm swimming.
A shower's just cleared, and the river's surface
fractures the low sun. Come join me, men.
Drop your ammunition belts and strip off
your fatigues. Dive in. Let your floating
prove you're more than stone, and can be held,
borne by water as we all were once.
Feel its pull, the stubborn tenderness
that will, in time, wear down the sharpest edge.
Above us, sliding raindrops find the tips
of leaves. Each one trembles, as if it mourns
the self it has to lose. Then it surrenders
to the fall, and there's nothing but light, and flow.

MOONLIGHT

Although I've invited you
here, to join me
in this poem's little room,
I can't speak your name.

I'm bound as tightly
as a priest, who draws
the curtain aside, and steps
out onto the cool stone floor.

So I must clip
my tongue, and do no more
than point towards the absent
care and many hurts,

the desolate unhealth
they left you with. Instead
I'll speak the heart of you, held
in a single photograph.

You'd just turned nineteen.
On house holiday, staff
and residents together.
Front seat of the minibus:

dark green anorak over
jim-jams, cigarette tucked
between your fingers, fringe
flicked clear of your eyes.

And yes—that waxing
crescent moon of a smile,
full of promise. *Give me
another chance* it beamed,

and always I succumbed,
being merely human.

THE BELL

Should you go back for real to that cherished place?
That refuge, conjured from the borderlands
of memory and fantasy, where faces
turn to welcome you, the barmaid's hand
already at the pump. The jukebox
with its litany of hits you know by heart.
The back door that no one ever locks,
though the world's kept firmly at bay, your hurts
anaesthetised. Let's hope it's been knocked down,
and a shopping mall's there instead. Better
that than the landlord's quizzical frown—
no, he doesn't remember you. Whatever
you now call home is miles away. They've rung
last orders. The night's no longer young.

BEING A BEAUTIFUL WOMAN

is like owning a dog. A dangerous
dog—one of those breeds the papers
go on about. Pit Bull. Rottweiler.

You take your dog for a walk,
and crowds part in front of you,
as if under some kind of spell.

Some people won't come near you.
They stand at a distance, hands
in pockets, stare at your dog.

Others make a big show of being
fearless. They stroke your dog
forcefully, speak to it too loudly.

If people talk to *you*, it's usually
about your dog. Some have dogs
themselves. Or wish they did.

You long to set your dog free,
for it to run around the park and lick
and dig and shit as it pleases.

But all your life you've been told
how lucky you are to own this dog.
It's criminal to neglect it.

You have to feed your dog with choice
cuts of meat, groom it, pamper it,
make it the centre of your world.

Above all else, you have to keep it
on a short leash. It's your fault
if somebody dies because of it.

LITTLE MACHINE

They say that talent skips a generation,
and you'd have agreed, looking at me, your son.
You who were happy grappling under a bonnet,
as deft at the wrench as the fine adjustment,
while I fumbled with a long screwdriver
trying to lever off a bicycle tyre.
The punctured inner tube was left more wounded.
The lunge of your blunt words: me, marooned
in a silence that no gauge could measure,
you with a face like a man in a seizure.
I sloped off, back to my exercise books
full of poems, long-handed in cursive loops.

The teenage me hid them up in the attic.
I played it cool, started playing music.
You said, years later—I'd not long turned thirty—
how, as a kid, you'd wanted to write poetry,
how the tireless grip of your mother's cold stare
stopped you dead, and I felt something stir,
a tick, or a pulse. You see, I've still no craft
with lathes, micrometers, drills. Here's my gift.
Listen to these words, their fit and throw,
this little machine that is breathing you,
its chittering valves and burnished tappets,
the cams in their endless, elliptical dance.

WATCH

Daybreak is gilding my bedroom window
though the night remains like a second skin.
Your tang and savour cling to my fingers
and lips. You're facing me but dead
to the world, to my neighbour opposite
shushing her cats downstairs, to the trucks
in the depot beyond the soccer pitch
announcing their slow reversal. I wonder how
this meeting could ever be thought of
as casual, when a lifetime of mistrust
and longing can pivot around every touch,
and it all comes down to that double-edged
word, the body not fully abandoned
to another through fear of being abandoned
by another. At least insomnia's gifted me
this: witnessing how sleep softens you,
how it lets your body slip free from its busily
managing self, leaving you flawlessly bare.
I feel compelled to watch, the way (they say)
a mother is, entranced by a dozing newborn.

Intimate stranger, I sense this won't end well.
Whatever I said, I brought you here to fix
a wound you can't heal. In a couple of hours
you'll get up, pull on yesterday's clothes, and all
of this will stay unspoken. What could you say,
anyway, if I told you my waking dream?
A baby lies still, framed by its cot, while
a woman is sluicing and clattering plates,
encased by a blank sadness. The child has turned
its head. Its gaze floats out through a window,
rises above a vegetable patch, a pair
of apple trees, the red roofs of an estate,
to a sky of no clouds, the sun a bowl
of boiling gold adrift in the limitless blue.

BREATH

—Merrywood Grammar, Knowle West, 1946

Pay attention! You must pay attention in class
Miss Davies snaps at the girl, just thirteen, staring
out through the window, though the girl's gaze
has already crossed the playground, the perimeter wall,
the valley beyond, and climbed the hill to the houses
on Bishopsworth Road. To one house, where a woman
with crippled lungs is lying in bed. The girl knows.
When she's sent to see the headmistress and explain,
she won't be believed, she'll be told she's being silly,
she'll be told her mother's going to be fine.
But the girl knows better, as she stares
at the house with its long garden path, along which
(five years before) she's running. The heavy drone
is getting louder. Across the city sirens are keening,
the sky in front of her above Dundry Hill is filling
with planes, and she runs past the neat rows
of carrots, potatoes, the wigwams of beans, then tumbles
down the steps into the shelter. She sits with her brother
and waits. At last, her parents. She hears the gurgle
and rasp of her mother's breath, drone, sirens,
thunder-thumps beginning in the middle distance.

The girl in the classroom knows it won't be long.
She imagines the tins on the dresser at home, lined
up strict as soldiers—GAS, ELECTRIC, PRUDENTIAL,
along to BUTCHER and MILK. Soon, it'll be her
who takes her father's hands, thick with money;
her who spreads the notes and coins on the table,
and portions them out. She thinks of the woman who smiles
from the side of the tins, her chocolate skin wrapped
in white cotton, her hand resting lightly on a tea bush
as if she were trying to soothe it. Back in the classroom
the girl knows all about waiting. She knows you can hold
your breath for the whole of your life. Her body is still.
You can't even see the rise and fall of her chest.

SIGNALMAN

There are worse lives I might have led
than his, witness to the seasons' slow
shift. Cotton grass, yellow flag,
bog myrtle, bulrush. Osprey, nightjar,
darter, snipe. Here the river parts its lips
to speak an estuary. The rails divide
and he's monarch of the marsh;
signals in three counties drop their arms
at his bidding. Block bells *ting-ting*
(train entering section: up stopping
from Aber). Reeds waver, salmon glint

then vanish. A constant lapping
of water, *Laver's Liverpool Tide Tables*
always to hand. He remembers
that January night. *A roar in the west,*
then half the Irish Sea fell out of the sky.
I saw the Gents go under like a U-boat
venting its tanks. 'Put your coat on Hughes,'
I said, 'it's time to go home'. On my hands
and knees I was, sleeper to sleeper,
pulling myself along the rails, waves
breaking about my ears—it was like
Waikiki beach out there.

I've been that man myself, of course,
stunned, bedraggled, wondering how
I'd survived the arrival of love. I've stared
at the wreckage, believing the flood
came out of the blue. But that's a lie:
wherever it was I crawled to for safety,
it's my heart that roared, my heart
the waters rose from.

VOICEMAIL

—for Kate

Although your mobile must be lying still
and unblinking on a bedside table

or stuffed in a bag with a pointless diary,
tonight I ring it one last time and hear

your voice, clear, unwavering, as you ask me
to *please leave a message after the tone*

and then I try to pretend you're busy,
writing songs on your scuffed acoustic, or down

in the lush, quiet county where you were born,
hands on the steering wheel's leopard-print cover,

casually speeding south through a warren
of hedge-bound lanes, stone bridges, up over

Eggardon Hill, to the place you'd go to stare
at the waves, breathe the incoming air.

COWLEY ROAD 3.30 PM

—Et in Arcadia ego

Rumours of further bombs start filtering through,
like the first skin-splashes before a storm breaks.
The screen re-loads. LONDON PARALYSED BY FEAR.
I notice my chest beginning to tighten.

I leave the office. In front of the clearance
shop opposite Tesco the three of us meet
by chance—me, the dancer, the Aeroplane Man
who once disabled an F1-11

with a hammer. There's just so much to discuss:
the best place to get your bicycle repaired;
dress code at forthcoming weddings; the amount
of drugs consumed at a recent festival.

Smiles are easy doves, fluttering round our heads,
and we could stand here all day if we wanted.
The air is hot, thick with fumes, but I breathe in
deeply, and try to feel my feet on the ground.

We part. I cycle down Cowley Road, mindful
of the oncoming buses as they swing out
to avoid the parked cars. It's a glorious
July afternoon. Anything might happen.

FLAME

Use matches sparingly
  —instruction on front of matchbox

Not meanness or thrift
but wisdom; respect
for each small torch
that's kept in there. Lover,

the same is true for words.
I bring you no fireworks.
A room is never so dark
that it needs more

than one slim burst
of sulphur to show
the mirror hung on its wall,
the way to its door.

And lovers know too
how even a single
flame might raise
a scar that time can't heal.

So come, stand next to me;
let's flip this little box.
Strike softly away from body.
See how it urges us.

VIA NEGATIVA

So if love's not a blazing yes
but the absence of a no

not the river itself but the lack
of a dam to halt its flow

then this is why the Tarot's Fool
is numbered with an O—

he steps off a cliff with sky above
and nothingness below

ABOUT THE AUTHOR

Originally from Merseyside, Alan Buckley moved to Oxford in the mid-1980s to study English Literature and has lived there ever since. Although he began writing poems and short stories at the age of eight, he stopped in his early teens and took up playing bass guitar. He went back to writing in his late 30s and his first pamphlet (*Shiver*) was a Poetry Book Society Choice in 2009. He won the Wigtown Prize in 2010, and was short-listed for the Picador Prize later that year. He has been highly commended in the Bridport Prize and Forward Prizes, as well as being widely published in magazines and anthologies. When his second pamphlet, *The Long Haul*, appeared from HappenStance in 2016, the first printing sold out in a matter of weeks. He was a school writer-in-residence with the charity First Story for eight years, and on the editorial board of ignition press from its inception in 2016 until 2019. He is a psychotherapist and for the last five years has specialised in trauma work with refugees. *Touched* is his first book-length collection.